COMMON
BUTTERFLIES
OF CALIFORNIA

COMMON
BUTTERFLIES
OF CALIFORNIA

Photography & Text by

Bob Stewart

WEST COAST LADY PRESS

1997

© 1998 by Bob Stewart

all rights reserved

Printed in Korea by Sung In Printing America, Inc.

10 9 8 7 6 5 4 3

West Coast Lady Press
P.O. Box 191
Patagonia
Arizona 85624

This book is dedicated to:

My wife Kathie Bunnell,
  artist,
    who reared many butterflies
    in Los Angeles in the 1940s

Samantha Stewart

Seth Bunnell

TABLE OF CONTENTS

GRASS SKIPPERS

CATERPILLARS (Larvae) OF SELECTED SPECIES

ACKNOWLEDGEMENTS

Ray Peterson rekindled my interest in butterflies. Debbie Perrin helped with the format, edited and typed earlier drafts. John Vernon (who has been collecting butterflies since he was a child in Texas) made important changes and additions. Liz Tuomi proof-read the final version of the manuscript. Claire Peaslee edited and crafted the manuscript toward publication readiness, for which I am very grateful.

PREFACE

For butterflies, there are several good field guides for the United States and California. For the most part, though, these guides have been produced by scientists who collect butterflies and who design their books to be used by others interested in collecting. There are a growing number of persons who are interested in identifying butterflies but do not want to kill them or even catch them in a net. With so many close-focusing binoculars (6-9 feet) available today, this is very easy to do. Of course one can watch butterflies with the unaided eye, but to get close you have to move very slowly.

One problem with current guides is that they often don't show the patterns on both the Under Wing and Upper Wing, something that is very necessary when all you have is a glimpse of just one side of the butterfly in the field. Also, these guides are rather overwhelming to beginners, with many look-alike species that do not occur in their local area.

As you gain experience, you will find butterly species that are not included in this book. But by becoming familiar with the common species, you will perhaps be motivated to obtain other guides, mentioned in the bibliography.

HOW TO USE THIS BOOK

This book has been organized by the following families:

Swallowtails: large butterflies with tails

Whites and Sulfurs: species that are predominantly white or yellow

Brush-footed Butterflies: a large group of diverse species that appear to have only four legs

Blues: small butterflies in which the males are blue on the Upper Wings

Hairstreaks: small butterflies that often have tiny tails on the Hind Wings

Coppers: small butterflies that generally have copper-colored Upper Wings

Skippers: small brown or blackish butterflies with the antennae clubs bent backward

For each species, a simple consistent format has been chosen to enable the user to obtain succinct information while referring to the photograph on the opposite page:

The common name is in bold letters, followed by the scientific name in italics.

KEY FIELD MARKS: The salient field marks that are distinguishing features for each species are given in boldface type. Because butterflies have two Front Wings and two Hind Wings, each side revealing different patterns, emphasis on field marks that most help in identifying the species is indicated by capitalized words.

SIZE: The size of the Front Wing, from the base to the tip, in inches.

ADULTS FLY: The months when the adult butterfly is seen. Sometimes a month is given in parentheses, which means it can be seen in that month also but not in large numbers.

HIBERNATE AS: Hibernation occurs in the winter months. The stage of hibernation, i.e., eggs, larvae, pupae, or adults, is given for each species.

HOST PLANTS: Listed are plant species on which each butterfly species will lay eggs, and which its larvae will eat.

RANGE: The general distribution of the species in California and elsewhere.

NOTES: An attempt has been made to give essential information as a starting point for knowledge of butterfly structure and behavior.

BUTTERFLY LIFE CYCLE

Butterflies deposit their eggs on discrete host plants. Some species lay only on one species of plant, while others may have quite a number of hosts. The egg is only a few millimeters in size; its surface is porous, with about 14,000 holes that allow air but not water to enter. The larva or caterpillar stage hatches from the egg and begins to eat the host plant. The butterfly larva, like all insects', has an outside skeleton or skin that eventually becomes too small for the growing caterpillar. It sheds this outer skin four or five times as it becomes larger, and three different hormones regulate this molting process. One of these, called juvenile hormone, keeps the larva from developing adult structures. This hormone does not circulate during the last molt, and some adult structures immediately begin to form on the inside of the caterpillar. When the last-stage caterpillar has grown to sufficient size, it wanders off to enter the pupa stage. In this stage, which results in an adult butterfly, there is a transformative chemical breakdown and reformation of all but certain thorax structures. The adult butterfly emerges from the pupal case and mates with its own species, and the female completes the cycle by laying her eggs on specific plants.

TECHNICAL NOTES

The common and scientific names are those used in the North American Butterfly Association Checklist and English Names of North American Butterflies by Cassie, *et al.* (1995). There are many named subspecies of butterflies: these are denoted by a third Latin name, e.g., *Hesperia comma dodgei*.

All but three of the photographs were taken with a Nikon 8008S body with a 105 macro lens (sometimes with a 4T diopter added) and a hand-held Nikon SB25 flash unit.

All photographs were taken under natural conditions.

BUTTERFLY SPECIES

WESTERN TIGER SWALLOWTAIL ▶ *Papillo rutulus*

KEY FIELD MARKS: Large butterfly with **four vertical black stripes** on **yellow**. Can be confused with Pale Swallowtail, but Pale has **cream**-colored wings.

SIZE: $3^{1}/_{2} - 4^{3}/_{8}$

ADULTS FLY: March through September

HIBERNATE AS: Pupae

HOST PLANTS: Willows (*Salix* spp.)
Alders (*Alnus* spp.)

RANGE: Throughout California and Western North America.

NOTES: All four Swallowtail species photographed here have two "tails" near their rear, a feature construed by bird predators as "antennae." In addition, in the first three species the brilliant red spots in iridescent blue are construed as "eye spots." In other words, it looks like the hind end of the butterfly is the head end. I have seen Steller's Jays go after this "tail end"; the butterfly flies away with the jay holding a "tail" in its beak. Notice how many Swallowtails (like the Anise Swallowtail photographed on page 6) have missing tails! Look objectively at the photographs and see which end is the most attractive to you.

PALE SWALLOWTAIL ▶ *Papillo eurymedon*

KEY FIELD MARKS: Large butterfly very similar to Tiger
Swallowtail but the four black vertical stripes
are on cream (not yellow).

SIZE: $3^3/_8 - 3^3/_4$

ADULTS FLY: May through June only

HIBERNATE AS: Pupae

HOST PLANTS: Cherry (*Prunus emarginata*)
(*Prunus ilicifolia*)
Ocean Spray (*Holodiscus discolor*)
California Coffeeberry (*Rhamnus californica*)
Red Berry (*Rhamnus crocea*)

RANGE: Throughout California and the western
United States.

NOTES: Males of many species of Swallowtails patrol
around hilltops waiting for females.

ANISE SWALLOWTAIL ▶ *Papilio zelicaon*

KEY FIELD MARKS: Large butterfly with black and yellow pattern. The top of the Front Wing has eight rectangles of yellow **surrounded by black** areas on both sides.

SIZE: 3 – 3 1/8

ADULTS FLY: March through September

HIBERNATE AS: Pupae

HOST PLANTS: Many carrot family species (*Apiaceae*)
Queen Anne's Lace (*Daucus carota*)
Poison Hemlock (*Conium maculatum*)
Fennel (*Foeniculum vulgare*)
Hog Fennels (*Lomatium californicum,*
L. dasycarpum, L. utriculatum)
Yampah (*Perideridia kelloggii*)

RANGE: Throughout California and the western United States.

NOTES: This species has profited from the introduction of Fennel, which grows readily in disturbed areas and has become the host plant most often used.

PIPEVINE SWALLOWTAIL ▶ *Battus philenor*

KEY FIELD MARKS: A Swallowtail with all blue Upper Wings, but note the Under Hind Wing pattern on page 10.

SIZE: $3 - 3\frac{1}{2}$

ADULTS FLY: April through September

HIBERNATE AS: Pupae

HOST PLANTS: California Pipevine (*Aristolochia californica*)

RANGE: Non-migratory population occurs in central California, but species occurs throughout eastern and southern United States.

NOTES: Adults are poisonous to birds because of chemicals derived from the larva, which eat California Pipevine. Nevertheless, even with this protection note the brighter color at the tails at the hind end that make the butterfly more attractive to bird predators. The adults have a tough body able to withstand bird bites.

PIPEVINE SWALLOWTAIL ▶ *Battus philenor*

Under Wing Pattern

In the eastern United States there are several species that are palatable to birds but that mimic the Under Wing pattern of the Pipevine Swallowtail, so predators leave them alone. This phenomenon is known as Batesian mimicry — when a palatable species mimics the color and pattern of a poisonous one. In order for this adaptation to succeed, there must be a good local population of the "model" species, e.g., Pipevine Swallowtails. Birds learn to avoid all patterns similar to the one that made them throw up.

This Swallowtail and others usually beat their front wings while nectaring. In such a large butterfly overheating could pose a problem. To reduce this possibility they cover the abdomen and fan the front wings while foraging.

This photo is of the Arizona subspecies.

CLODIUS PARNASSIAN ▶ *Parnassius clodius*

KEY FIELD MARKS: A large white butterfly with **red spots** on the Hind Wings and **all black** antennae.

SIZE: $1^7/_8 - 2^7/_8$

ADULTS FLY: June through August

HIBERNATE AS: Eggs

HOST PLANTS: Bleeding Heart (*Dicentra formosa*)

RANGE: Coast Range (Mendocino County northward) and west slopes of the Sierra Nevada/Cascade Range. Restricted to the western United States.

NOTES: The host plants (*Dicentra* spp.) contain poisonous alkaloids which probably make the butterfly poisonous as well. Many white butterflies are poisonous to predators such as birds (perhaps because white is a very visible color to utilize as a warning).

A closely related alpine species called the Phoebus Parnassian (*Parnassius phoebus*) can best be differentiated from Clodius by the **black and white** antennae and red spots on the Front Wing (as well as on the Hind Wing).

CLODIUS PARNASSIAN ▶ *Parnassius clodius*

Notice the black base to the wing and the black body designed for good heat absorption. The abdomen of this individual is large, so it could be a female (females have larger abdomens for egg production). Males capture females by grabbing them in mid-air. After mating, the male leaves a white plug (*sphragis*) in the female's cloacal opening so she cannot mate with another male.

CABBAGE WHITE ▶ *Pieris rapae*

KEY FIELD MARKS: A white butterfly with **solid grey tips** to the Front Wing. Can be confused with Veined White, which has black-edged veins and **not a solid** grey tip to Front Wing.

SIZE: $1^5/_8 - 2^1/_4$

ADULTS FLY: Early spring to fall

HIBERNATE AS: Pupae

HOST PLANTS: Many mustard family plants including:
Black Mustard (*Brassica nigra*)
Summer Mustard (*Brassica geniculata*)
Wild Radish (*Raphanus sativus*)
Garden Cabbage
Nasturtium

RANGE: Throughout North America.

NOTES: Mustard oils derived from the host plants are poisonous to birds. Females can live up to three weeks and can lay up to 700 eggs!

In this photograph, the female (the whiter individual) can be distinguished by **three** black spots showing through the Under Hind Wing (male only has **two** spots).

MUSTARD (VEINED) WHITE ▶ *Pieris napi*

KEY FIELD MARKS: All white butterfly without a solid gray tip to Front Wings and **dark** around veins on Under Hind Wings.

SIZE: $1\frac{1}{2}$ – 2

ADULTS FLY: February through June

HIBERNATE AS: Pupae

HOST PLANTS: Many mustard family species (*Brassicacae*) Milkmaids (*Cardamine californica*)

RANGE: Especially common in wooded canyons. Not found in the southern half of California. Western and northern portions of North America.

NOTES: The mustard oils derived from host plants make this species poisonous to birds.

SARA ORANGETIP ▶ *Anthocharis sara*

KEY FIELD MARKS: A small white with **orange tips** on the Front Wing (note the yellow veins and greenish spots on the Under Hind Wing)

SIZE: $1^1/_4 - 1^7/_8$

ADULTS FLY: February through June

HIBERNATE AS: Pupae

HOST PLANTS: Hedge Mustard (*Sisymbrium officinale*)
Rock Cress (*Arabis* spp.)
Western Tansy Mustard (*Descurainia pinnata*)
Lace Pod (*Thysanocarpus curvipes*)
Field Mustard (*Brassica campestris*)

RANGE: All over California. Western United States.

NOTES: Males patrol all day looking for females, stopping occasionally for a few seconds to sip nectar. Photo opportunities for males are rare: the only time they remain still for more than a few seconds is when courting a female. This photo is of a female.

ORANGE SULFUR ▶ *Colias eurytheme*

KEY FIELD MARKS: A **yellow** butterfly with orange tints. Upper Wing has a black border; Under Hind Wing usually has a silver spot with a red rim and a smaller spot next to it. (Often the females are white or greenish, as shown in this photograph of a mated pair.)

SIZE: $1^{3}/_{4} - 2^{3}/_{8}$

ADULTS FLY: Spring to fall

HIBERNATE AS: Larvae

HOST PLANTS: Birds Foot Trefoil (*Lotus scoparius*)
Hill Lotus (*Lotus subpinnatus*)
Lupines (*Lupinus succulentus, L. bicolor*)
Sweet Clovers (*Melilotus officinalis, M. alba*)
California Tea (*Psoralea*)
Clovers (*Trifolium repens, T. tridentata,* and *T. wormskjoldii*)
Vetches (*Vicia americana, V. angustifolia*)
Alfalfa (*Medicago sativa*)

RANGE: All over California and throughout North America.

NOTES: Like the Cabbage White that grows on vegetable crops, the Orange Sulfur has become a common butterfly because it can use Alfalfa as a host plant.

CALIFORNIA DOGFACE ▶ *Colias eurydice*

KEY FIELD MARKS: Front Wing **pointed** at the tip; Under Hind Wing with two circles. (Note the "dog face" showing through the Under Front Wing; the spot on the Front Wing is the "eye").

SIZE: $2 - 2^{1}/_{4}$

ADULTS FLY: April through September

HIBERNATE AS: Pupae

HOST PLANTS: False Indigo (*Amorpha californica*)

RANGE: Throughout California at low elevations where food plant is available but not in the southern deserts.

NOTES: This is the California state butterfly.

CLOUDLESS SULFUR ▶ *Phoebis sennae*

KEY FIELD MARKS: The male is a **large** bright yellow butterfly (see notes below on female).

SIZE: $2^{1}/_{2} - 2^{3}/_{4}$

ADULTS FLY: April through May

HIBERNATE AS: Pupae

HOST PLANTS: Senna (*Cassia* spp.)

RANGE: Mostly in the desert regions of southern California and all over the southern half of the United States.

NOTES: Sulfurs rarely perch with open wings. This photograph is of the female. Note the two circular marks on the Under Hind Wing (and also on the Under Front Wing). Notice also the faint **wavy diagonal brownish lines** that form an **offset** pattern on both Under Wings.

GULF FRITILLARY ▶ *Agraulis vanillae*

KEY FIELD MARKS: Long orange brown Upper Wing with a triangle of three spots that are white surrounded by black.

SIZE: $2^5/_8 - 3^1/_8$

ADULTS FLY: March through November

HIBERNATE AS: Pupae

HOST PLANTS: Passion Flower (*Passiflora* spp.)

RANGE: Coastal California, southern Texas and Florida, south to Argentina. It is now a resident of Hawaii.

NOTES: This butterfly belongs to a tropical group known as Long-wings. There are about 500 species of *Passiflora* in the tropics. Most *Passiflora* species that serve as the host plant for the Long-wings contain an organic cyanide compound that is poisonous to birds.

GULF FRITILLARY ▶ *Agraulis vanillae*

Under Wing with silver spots

The introduction of *Passiflora* species has led to the expansion of the Gulf Fritillary's range into northern California. The silver spots reflect ultraviolet light, which we cannot see but which is visible to the butterflies.

GREAT SPANGLED FRITILLARY ▶ *Speyeria cybele leto*

KEY FIELD MARKS: **Under Hind Wing** with a **wide** lighter band near the margin, contrasting with the darker inner part of the wing containing small silvery spots.

SIZE: $2^7/_8 - 3^1/_8$

ADULTS FLY: July through August

HIBERNATE AS: Unfed first-stage larvae

HOST PLANTS: Violets (*Viola* spp.)

RANGE: Subspecies *leto* is found in middle elevations on both sides of the Cascade/Sierra Nevada mountains and throughout the northern United States. There are about eight other subspecies.

NOTES: The photograph is of a male (note the bright orange Upper Wing; the female is black and white on the Upper Wing). Fritillary species are difficult for the beginner to distinguish because of their very similar appearance.

CALLIPPE FRITILLARY ▶ *Speyeria callippe nevadensis*

KEY FIELD MARKS: The inner two-thirds of the Under Hind Wing is greenish with large silvery spots.

SIZE: $2 - 2\frac{1}{8}$

ADULTS FLY: June through July

HIBERATE AS: Unfed first-stage larvae

HOST PLANTS: Johnny Jump-ups (*Viola pedunculata*)

RANGE: The subspecies is found east of the Sierra/Cascade crest. There are several other subspecies. Together they range throughout California.

NOTES: This photograph was taken just east of Monitor Pass, California.

HYDASPE FRITILLARY ▶ *Speyeria hydaspe*

KEY FIELD MARKS: This individual, photographed on the east side of the Sierra Nevada in Plumas National Forest near Quincy, has **Under Hind Wing** with a **maroon** ground color and **ivory** (unsilvered) spots.

SIZE: $2 - 2^3/8$

ADULTS FLY: June through August

HIBERNATE AS: Unfed first-stage larvae

HOST PLANTS: Violets (*Viola* spp.)

RANGE: Sierra Nevada/Cascade Range and midwestern to northwestern United States.

PACIFIC FRITILLARY ▶ *Boloria epithore*

KEY FIELD MARKS: A **small** Fritillary with a purplish cast on the
Under Hind Wing

SIZE: $1^5/_8 - 1^7/_8$

ADULTS FLY: Mid-May through June

HIBERNATE AS: Fourth-stage larvae

HOST PLANTS: Violets (*Viola* spp.)

RANGE: Sierra Nevada/Cascade Range, Coast Range,
and northwestern United States.

AMERICAN LADY ▶ *Vanessa virginiensis*

This is a close-up showing the characteristic three legs on one side of a "True" brush-footed butterfly. Note the front leg is severely reduced. This leg is not used for walking or perching but for testing the chemistry of the plant. When landing, the female flashes these tiny legs out to touch the plant. If she determines that this is a suitable host plant, she may lay her eggs.

CALIFORNIA PATCH ▶ *Chlosyne californica*

KEY FIELD MARKS: Similar to the Bordered Patch (page 44) with a wide band in the middle of the Upper Wing, but the California Patch has a thinner **second band** along the outer edge.

SIZE: $1\frac{1}{4} - 1\frac{3}{4}$

ADULTS FLY: March through April (to November)

HIBERNATE AS: Third-stage larvae

HOST PLANTS: Desert Sunflower (*Viguiera deltoides*)

RANGE: Southern California and extreme southwestern United States and Baja California.

BORDERED PATCH ▶ *Chlosyne lacinia*

KEY FIELD MARKS:	A wide orange band on Upper Wing surrounded on **both sides** with dark brown
SIZE:	$1^1/_2 - 1^3/_4$
ADULTS FLY:	March through October
HIBERNATE AS:	Third-stage larvae
HOST PLANTS:	Sunflower (*Helianthus annus* var. *lenticularis*)
RANGE:	Extreme southern California and southwestern United States
NOTES:	This individual was imbibing nutrients from mammal dung.

VARIABLE CHECKERSPOT ▶ *Euphydryas chalcedona*

KEY FIELD MARKS: A black butterfly with a multitude of yellow spots and smaller red spots on the Upper Front Wing. Note the **white dots** on the back of the abdomen.

SIZE: $1^1/_2 - 2^1/_8$

ADULTS FLY: April through June

HIBERNATE AS: Larvae

HOST PLANTS: Sticky Monkey Bush (*Mimulus aurantiacus*) California Bee Plant (*Scrophularia californica*) Indian Warrior (*Pedicularis densiflorus*) English Plantain (*Plantago lanceolata*)

RANGE: Throughout California as several named subspecies. Western United States.

NOTES: Average adult life span nine to ten days. Larvae, pupae and adults are poisonous to vertebrates. During droughts, larvae can hibernate for several years!

VARIABLE CHECKERSPOT ▶ *Euphydryas chalcedona*

Underwings

Note that there are more extensive **creamy spots** in the **Under Front Wing** compared to the Northern Checkerspot (page 54).

LEANIRA CHECKERSPOT ▶ *Thessalia leanira*

KEY FIELD MARKS: Male (this photograph) has dark Upper
Wing; red streaks at base (outer edge) of
Upper Front Wing. Under Hind Wing of
both sexes has prominent dark band with
enclosed spots. Note the white **stripes** on the
abdomen.

SIZE: $1^3/_8 - 1^3/_4$

ADULTS FLY: April through June

HIBERNATE AS: Third-stage larvae

HOST PLANTS: Paintbrush (*Castilleja* spp.)

RANGE: Throughout California and the western
United States.

NORTHERN CHECKERSPOT ▶ *Chlosyne palla*

KEY FIELD MARKS:	A Checkerspot that has a **yellowish band** running through **both** Upper Wings but lacks the round spots and crescents near the edge of the Upper Hind Wings of the Mylitta and Field Crescents (see pages 56 and 58).
SIZE:	$1^3/_8 - 1^7/_8$
ADULTS FLY:	May through July
HIBERNATE AS:	Half-grown larvae
HOST PLANTS:	Paintbrush (*Castilleja* spp.)
RANGE:	In California found mostly in the central and northern portions. Western United States.

NORTHERN CHECKERSPOT ▶ *Chlosyne palla*

Under Wing

Note the lack of numerous creamy spots (only one row) in the Under Front Wing, compared to Variable Checkerspot (page 48).

MYLITTA CRESCENT ▶ *Phyciodes mylitta*

KEY FIELD MARKS: A relatively small butterfly with small crescents with black dots above them near the margin of the Upper Hind Wing. The leading edge of the Upper Front Wing has four vertical bars — the two outer ones are solid black, and the two inner ones have orange in the middle but dark outlines.

SIZE: $1^{1}/_{8} - 1^{5}/_{8}$

ADULTS FLY: March through October

HIBERNATE AS: Half-grown larvae

HOST PLANTS: Thistles:
Bull Thistle (*Cirsium vulgare*)
Cobweb Thistle (*Cirsium occidentale*)
Milk Thistle (*Silybum marianum*)
Italian Thistle (*Carduus pycnocephalus*)

RANGE: Throughout California. Western United States.

NOTES: This small butterfly seems to be always in motion, even when perched. Its habit of flying out to contact other insects and butterflies appears to be territorial behavior, but the Crescent is really just checking to see if the other is one of its own kind. Males perch on weeds or grass and inspect all passing butterflies, looking for females. Like all butterflies, they see motion very well from a distance but have to be very close to recognize their own species pattern.

FIELD CRESCENT ▶ *Phyciodes campestris*

KEY FIELD MARKS: Upper Wing **dark** with yellow-orange band

SIZE: $1\frac{1}{4} - 1\frac{5}{8}$

ADULTS FLY: April through October

HIBERNATE AS: Half-grown larvae

HOST PLANTS: California Aster (*Aster californicus*)
Aster (*Aster chilensis*)

RANGE: In central and northern California but not in southern California. Western United States.

NOTES: This species and the Mylitta Crescent can be told from the other Checkerspots here (Variable, Leanira, Northern and Tiny) by the marks on their Upper Hind Wing — dark circles near the edges and the crescents.

TINY CHECKERSPOT ▶ *Dymasia dymas chara*

KEY FIELD MARKS:	A small Checkerspot with a pale median band on Upper Front Wing. The Under Hind Wing margin has a **black marginal line** and white spots (in the facing photograph, see the one butterfly revealing Under Hind Wing).
SIZE:	$7/8 - 1 1/8$
ADULTS FLY:	March through April and September through October
HIBERNATE AS:	Pupae
HOST PLANTS:	Chuperosa (*Justicia californica*)
RANGE:	Southern California deserts and southern Arizona

SATYR COMMA ▶ *Polygonia satyrus*

KEY FIELD MARKS:	An orange and black butterfly with naturally cut-out wing edges. (See pages 65-66 for comparison to Hoary Comma.)
SIZE:	$1^7/_8 - 2^3/_8$
ADULTS FLY:	All year
HIBERNATE AS:	Adults
HOST PLANTS:	Nettle (*Urtica holosericea*)
RANGE:	Throughout California but rare in the deserts. Western and northern United States.
NOTES:	Males spend much time patrolling sunny glades looking for females.

SATYR COMMA ▶ *Polygonia satyrus*

Under Wings

Note the resemblance to a dead leaf, complete with cut-out
edges, the silvery "comma" (each end comes to a point), and the
very small front leg extending near the back of the butterfly's eye.
This individual is sipping fluid from a muddy path to obtain nutri-
ent salts. (See American Lady *Vanessa virginiensis*, page 40.)
Although the Satyr Comma's Under Wing is darker at the base and
thus has a two-toned appearance, the outer portion is **light brown**,
not **grayish white** as in the Hoary Comma.

HOARY COMMA ▶ *Polygonia gracilis zephyrus*

KEY FIELD MARKS: The three Upper Front Wing **inner spots** are all single spots (see Satyr Comma, page 62, which has the lower spot doubled). Under Wing has lighter, whitish-gray outer half; the white "comma" is thin throughout.

SIZE: $1\frac{1}{2} - 1\frac{7}{8}$

ADULTS FLY: Late June through September

HIBERNATE AS: Adults

HOST PLANTS: Currant (*Ribes* spp.)

RANGE: Subspecies *zephyrus* is in California. Western North America.

CALIFORNIA TORTOISESHELL ▶ *Nymphalis californica*

KEY FIELD MARKS: A medium-sized orange butterfly with dark borders all around the Upper Wing. There are three large irregular shapes along the leading edge of the Upper Front Wing; the outer one is bordered on two sides with white.

SIZE: $2 - 2^3/_8$

ADULTS FLY: All year (but mainly February to early April)

HIBERNATE AS: Adults

HOST PLANTS: California Lilac (*Ceanothus thrysiflorus*)
Buckbrush (*Ceanothus cuneatus*)

RANGE: Throughout California (rare in southern deserts). Western United States.

NOTES: This species hibernates in the winter until warm weather arrives in early spring. Overwintering individuals lay eggs and die. The second generation becomes adult in late May to early June, migrating to the Sierra where two more broods are produced. Individuals from the last-summer broods migrate back to lowland California to hibernate in winter.

MOURNING CLOAK ▶ *Nymphalis antiopa*

KEY FIELD MARKS:	A large dark butterfly with a yellow border to the Upper Wing.
SIZE:	$2^3/_4 - 3^1/_2$
ADULTS FLY:	March through August
HIBERNATE AS:	Adult
HOST PLANTS:	Willows (*Salix* spp.) Poplars (*Populus* spp.) Alders (*Alnus* spp.)
RANGE:	Throughout California and North America.

AMERICAN LADY ▶ *Vanessa virginiensis*

KEY FIELD MARKS: An orange and black butterfly with a white rectangle on the leading edge of the Upper Front Wing (similar to Painted Lady) and a **small white spot** in orange on the edge of the Upper Front Wing. The Upper Hind Wing spots are generally merged, and only two are blue-centered.

SIZE: $1^3/4 - 2^1/2$

ADULTS FLY: All year

HIBERNATE AS: Adults

HOST PLANTS: Prefers Sunflower family:
Cudweeds (*Gnaphalium palustre,*
G. purpureum)
Pearly Everlasting (*Anaphalis margaritacea*)
Mugwort (*Artemisia douglasiana*)
Milk Thistle (*Silybum marianum*)

RANGE: Throughout California, North America, and Mexico (and south).

AMERICAN LADY ▶ *Vanessa virginiensis*

Unlike the Painted Lady and the West Coast Lady, the American Lady's Under Hind Wing has only **two** large, round spots. Note the **white** spot **in orange** on the Front Wing.

PAINTED LADY ▶ *Vanessa cardui*

KEY FIELD MARKS: Orange and black butterfly with **white rectangle** (three spots run together) on outer leading edge of Front Wing. Four Upper Hind Wing spots are **all black**.

SIZE: $2 - 2^{3}/_{4}$

ADULTS FLY: All year

HIBERNATE AS: Adults

HOST PLANTS: Mostly thistles:
Bull Thistle (*Cirsium vulgare*)
Cobweb Thistle (*Cirsium occidentale*)
Milk Thistle (*Silybum marianum*)
Yellow Star Thistle (*Centaurea solstitialis*)
Yarrow (*Achillea millefolium*)
Pearly Everlasting (*Anaphalis margaritacea*)
Mule Ears (*Wyethia glabra*)
Cheeseweed (*Malva nicaensis*)
Alfalfa (*Medicago sativa*)
English Plantain (*Plantago lanceolata*)

RANGE: Throughout California, North America, and Mexico. This butterfly has the widest range of any species in the world. Can be common during spring migration.

NOTES: In California there is a strong migration north in late March through April, but one not so strong (if any) to the south in the fall.

WEST COAST LADY ▶ *Vanessa annabella*

KEY FIELD MARKS: An orange and black butterfly with an orange rectangle on the leading edge of the Upper Front Wing. The four Upper Hind Wing spots are filled with blue.

SIZE: $1^3/_4 - 2^1/_8$

ADULTS FLY: All year

HIBERNATE AS: Adults

HOST PLANTS: Cheeseweed (*Malva nicaensis*)
Western Hollyhock (*Sidalcea malvaeflora*)
Lupines (*Lupinus succulentus, L. arboreus*)
Other Mallow family species, Malvaceae

RANGE: Throughout California and the western United States.

NOTES: See cover for photograph of Under Wing, showing four prominent spots (and a fainter fifth).

RED ADMIRAL ▶ *Vanessa atalanta*

KEY FIELD MARKS: An orange and black butterfly with a **broad orange band** on the Upper Front Wing and an orange band at the bottom of the Upper Hind Wing.

SIZE: $2 - 2^5/_8$

ADULTS FLY: All year

HIBERNATE AS: Adults

HOST PLANTS: Nettle (*Urtica holosericea*)

RANGE: Throughout California and North America, especially in willow and forest habitats where Nettle is abundant.

Under Wings

This individual is sipping nutrients from dung. Note the **lack of round spots** on the Under Hind Wing. The other Ladies (*Vanessa* spp.) have spots.

COMMON BUCKEYE ▶ *Junonia coenia*

KEY FIELD MARKS: Unique set of **large eye spots** on Upper Wing and **two orange rectangles** on leading edge of Upper Front Wing.

SIZE: $1^5/_8 - 2^1/_4$

ADULTS FLY: All year

HIBERNATE AS: Larvae

HOST PLANTS: English Plantain (*Plantago lanceolata*)
Dwarf Plantain (*Plantago erecta*)
Seep Spring Mimulus (*Mimulus guttatus*)
Owls Clover (*Orthocarpus purpurascens*)
Speedwell (*Veronica americana*)
Mat Grass (*Lippia nodiflora*)

RANGE: Throughout California and the United States.

NOTES: The large eye spot on the Upper Front Wing is surrounded by white, with a band continuing into the upper part of the wing that reflects ultraviolet light. The eye spots may scare away young birds, but the number of individuals seen with these spots missing argues that some birds are fooled to think they are real eyes. I have seen many individuals flying well with several of the eye spots missing. In California the species does not migrate. Adults live for only ten days. Males spend most of their time patrolling for females along trails and fire roads in grassy or weedy areas.

LORQUIN'S ADMIRAL ▶ *Limenitis lorquini*

KEY FIELD MARKS: A large black and white butterfly with an orange tip on the Upper Front Wing. (California Sister similar but with black tip to the Upper Front Wing).

SIZE: $2^1/_8 - 2^7/_8$

ADULTS FLY: April to October

HIBERNATE AS: Half-grown larvae in a rolled leaf

HOST PLANTS: Willows (*Salix* spp.)
Bitter Cherry (*Prunus emarginata*)
Ocean Spray (*Holodiscus discolor*)
Western Choke Cherry (*Prunus demissa*)

RANGE: Throughout California and extreme western United States.

NOTES: The larvae look like bird droppings (see page 246). Found usually along streams where Willows grow.

LORQUIN'S ADMIRAL ▶ *Limenitis lorquini*

Under Wing

The white stripe in the wing reflects ultraviolet light, which has a shorter wavelength than the blue that we can detect. However, butterflies can see ultraviolet, so by reflecting it they can attract their own kind. A similar stripe exists in the California Sister (page 90).

CALIFORNIA SISTER ▶ *Adelpha bredowii*

KEY FIELD MARKS: A large butterfly with a large orange area **near** the tip of the Upper Front Wing, but note the **tip is dark**. (Like Lorquin's Admiral but tip is orange in that species.)

SIZE: $2^3/_8 - 3^1/_2$

ADULTS FLY: April through October

HIBERNATE AS: Larvae

HOST PLANTS: Oaks (*Quercus chrysolepis, Q. agrifolia, Q. kelloggii*) and others

RANGE: Throughout California and the western United States.

NOTES: This species (and Lorquin's Admiral) fly with a particular flap and glide pattern reminiscent of the flight of Sharp-shinned Hawks.

This photograph was taken in Great Basin National Park, Utah.

Under Wing

This species has been especially difficult to approach for close-up views. The photograph opposite was taken after several days of rain in May.

Once while attempting to photograph California Sisters in a small creek on the western slope of the Sierra Nevada, I was unable to get close, but to my surprise one of the butterflies alighted on my camera lens. It dabbed with its proboscis, perhaps getting needed salts. Repeatedly it would fly off and come back. Subsequently I used this individual perched on my lens as a decoy to approach very close to other individuals.

CALIFORNIA RINGLET ▶ *Coenonympha tullia california*

KEY FIELD MARKS: A moth look-a-like but with **clubbed antennae** (characteristic of most butterflies). Tiny **rings of black** on wings, thus the name Ringlet.

SIZE: $1 - 1\frac{1}{4}$

ADULTS FLY: March through October

HIBERNATE AS: Larvae

HOST PLANTS: Grasses:
Purple Needle Grass (*Nassella pulchra*)
Bluegrass (*Poa pratensis*)

RANGE: Throughout California. Many other subspecies are found throughout northern North America.

COMMON WOOD-NYMPH ▶ *Cercyonis pegala*

KEY FIELD MARKS: A dark, medium-sized butterfly with two large eye spots (the upper spot is **slightly** smaller than the lower) on the Under Front Wing. Note the **darker band** on the **inner part** of the Underwing.

SIZE: $1^7/_8 - 2^3/_4$

ADULTS FLY: June through July

HIBERNATE AS: Unfed larvae

HOST PLANTS: Grasses

RANGE: Throughout North America as several subspecies. Not found in the Central Valley or southern California.

NOTES: This species and the Ringlet, plus the other species through page 104, are representative of a group of butterflies called Satyrs. Characteristic of the group are the eye spots, which draw the attention of a predator away from the head end. This group is not poisonous and relies on its unique, evasive flutter-flight and dull colors for protection against bird predators.

GREAT BASIN WOOD-NYMPH ▶ *Cercyonis sthenele sylvestris*

KEY FIELD MARKS: Front Wing **upper spot larger** than the lower (in males but not females). The band on the inner part of the Under Wing is not as dark as in the Common Wood-Nymph (page 96).

SIZE: $1^3/_4 - 2$

ADULTS FLY: May through August

HIBERNATE AS: Unfed first-stage larvae

HOST PLANTS: Grasses

RANGE: Throughout California (except the Central Valley) and the western United States.

SMALL WOOD-NYMPH ▶ *Cercyonis oetus*

KEY FIELD MARKS: Upper Front Wing eye spot **much larger** than the lower; the lower much closer to the wing edge. **Zig-zag dark lines** on **dark** Under Hind Wing.

SIZE: $1^1/_2 - 1^7/_8$

ADULTS FLY: Late June through August

HIBERNATE AS: Unfed first-stage larvae

HOST PLANTS: Grasses

RANGE: In northern California, east of the Sierra Nevada/Cascade Range. Western United States.

CHRYXUS ARCTIC ▶ *Oeneis chryxus*

KEY FIELD MARKS:	Under Hind Wing with a dark middle band often bordered by white on the outside.
SIZE:	$1^{3}/_{4} - 2^{1}/_{4}$
ADULTS FLY:	Mid-July to mid-August
HIBERNATE AS:	Larvae
HOST PLANTS:	Grasses
RANGE:	High Sierra Nevada (Inyo County north to Donner Pass).
NOTES:	This species is found mostly in alternate years (odd-numbered years), as it takes two years to develop into the adult stage.

RIDINGS' SATYR ▶ *Neominois ridingsii*

KEY FIELD MARKS: Zig-zag dark lines on **light** Under Hind Wing. Upper dark spot (hardly showing in this photograph) on Under Front Wing is in **light** ground-colored area, with a **zig-zag line** near the outer edge of the wing.

SIZE: $1^1/_2 - 2$

ADULTS FLY: July through August

HIBERNATE AS: Young larvae

HOST PLANTS: Grasses

RANGE: High Sierra Nevada and White Mountains in eastern California. Western United States.

NOTES: This species is found mostly in alternate years (even-numbered years), as it takes two years to develop into the adult stage.

MONARCH ▶ *Danaus plexippus*

KEY FIELD MARKS: A large orange butterfly that has a black body and black borders to the Upper Wing.

SIZE: $4^1/_8 - 4^5/_8$

ADULTS FLY: All year

HIBERNATE AS: Adults

HOST PLANTS: Milkweed species (*Asclepias* spp.)

RANGE: Throughout California. North America and Mexico.

NOTES: California Monarch adults mate in late winter. Overwintering adults then migrate from coastal wintering spots to find Milkweed species. After laying eggs, these adults die. At least four more generations can occur until fall, when that generation flies to traditional California coastal sites (where these individuals have never been before) and lives up to eight months. The summer-generation adults live only a couple of weeks. The larvae that eat poisonous Milkweed (not all species of Milkweed plants have the poisonous chemical) are poisonous to birds. The poison is stored mostly in the butterfly's exoskeleton. Some birds have learned to strip the exoskeleton off to eat the internal muscles and abdomen. The Queen and Viceroy butterflies are also poisonous. Together with the Monarch they form a Mullerian Mimicry complex. Birds learn that the pattern is not good to eat, thus protecting all three species once they have tasted one.

Showing the Under Wings.

QUEEN ▶ *Danaus gilippus*

KEY FIELD MARKS:	Similar to the Monarch but with **white spots** in the orange of the Upper Front Wing.
SIZE:	$2^3/_4 - 3^1/_2$
ADULTS FLY:	April through November
HIBERNATE AS:	Pupae
HOST PLANTS:	Milkweed species (*Asclepias* spp.) Climbing Milkweed (*Sarcostemma* spp.)
RANGE:	Southern half of North America. In California it is found in the desert regions and occasionally in the Great Basin east of the Sierra Nevada.
NOTES:	Pheromones play a key role in the life of the Queen butterfly. The male stores the chemical in glands on its Upper Hind Wing, close to both sides of the abdomen. (See the dark glands on the Upper Hind Wing of the male Monarch, pictured on page 106.) But first he must manufacture the pheromone from alkaloids that he draws from dead leaves of Heliotrope (*Heliotropium* sp.) and other plants. With the alkaloids, he synthesizes the pheromone necessary to attract the female and stores a large amount of just the alkaloids. When mating he delivers the stored alkaloids to the female along with his sperm. The alkaloids, known to be poisonous to predators, are passed on in the eggs, larvae and future adults. Additional protection against predators is given by a different chemical in the Milkweed host plants.

Showing the **white spots on orange** in the Under Front Wing.

SPRING AZURE ▶ *Celastrina ladon echo*

KEY FIELD MARKS: Under Hind Wing has a rather dull pattern compared to other blues. Note the faint V's and faint dots on the outer edges of the Under Hind Wing.

SIZE: $1 - 1\frac{1}{8}$

ADULTS FLY: February through July

HIBERNATE AS: Pupae

HOST PLANTS: Chamise (*Adenostoma fasciculatum*)
Ocean Spray (*Holodiscus discolor*)
California Buckeye (*Aesculus californica*)
California Lilac (*Ceanothus* spp)
Creek Dogwood (*Cornus occidentalis*)

RANGE: Throughout California (*echo*) and the United States (*echo* and other subspecies)

NOTES: In the early spring this species is attracted to mud, where the butterflies congregate in large numbers to sip moisture. Males fly around bushes and small trees searching for females.

ACMON BLUE ▶ *Plebejus acmon acmon*

KEY FIELD MARKS: Five to six **large** orange spots near the margin of the Under Hind Wing **only**. The black circles on the Under Wing have **silvery caps** on their outer edges.

The Dotted Blue (*Euphilotes enoptes bayensis*) and the Square-spotted Blue (*Euphilotes battoides*) also have orange spots only on the Under Hind Wing but lack the silvery caps above the black circles (see page 117).

SIZE: $^3/_4 - 1$

ADULTS FLY: March through October

HIBERNATE AS: Larvae

HOST PLANTS: Shrubs and herbs of Buckwheat and Pea families:
Eriogonums (*Eriogonum latifolium, E. nudum*)
Field Knotweed (*Polygonum aviculare*)
Birds Foot Tree Foil (*Lotus scoparius*)
Lotus (*Lotus humistratus*)
Spanish Lotus (*Lotus purshianus*)
Small Flowered Lotus (*Lotus micranthus*)
White Sweet Clover (*Melilotus alba*)

RANGE: Throughout California (*acmon*) and the western United States (*acmon* and other subspecies).

NOTES: While nectaring, this species moves its Hind Wings like some Hairstreaks do, to draw attention to its orange "eye spots." A bird predator will bite the Hind Wing thus missing the head end, and the butterfly escapes.

SQUARE-SPOTTED BLUE ▶ *Euphilotes battoides*

KEY FIELD MARKS: Under Wing spots (especially on Under Front Wing) **squarish**; reddish band on Under Hind Wing.

SIZE: $^3/_4 - 1$

ADULTS FLY: March through August

HIBERNATE AS: Pupae

HOST PLANTS: Buckwheat (*Eriogonum* spp.)

RANGE: Throughout California except on the central and north coast and in the Central Valley. Western United States.

NOTES: Not always with squarish spots, so can be very similar to the Dotted Blue (*Euphilotes enoptes*). Photographed at Sonora Pass.

MELISSA BLUE ▶ *Lycaeides melissa*

KEY FIELD MARKS: The orange spots are **fused** to form a continuous band on **both** Under Wings.

SIZE: $1 - 1\frac{1}{4}$

ADULTS FLY: Mid-May through July

HIBERNATE AS: Eggs

HOST PLANTS: Loco Weed (*Astragalus* spp.)
Lupines (*Lupinus* spp.)

RANGE: East of Sierra Nevada crest and in southern California.

NOTES: Similar to the Anna's Blue (*Lycaeides idas anna*), but the orange spots in Anna's are absent or very small and so **do not form a continuous band**. Females of both forms have orange band on **both** Upper Wings (*melissa* has **broader** band on Front Wing). Photographed at Kit Carson Pass.

SILVERY BLUE ▶ *Glaucopsyche lygdamus*

KEY FIELD MARKS:	Only **one** row of dots on the Under Hind Wing (with a broad white ring around each dark dot).
SIZE:	$1 - 1^{1}/_{4}$
ADULTS FLY:	March through May
HIBERNATE AS:	Pupae
HOST PLANTS:	Birds Foot Tree Foil (*Lotus scoparius*) Spanish Lotus (*Lotus purshianus*) Lupines (*Lupinus micranthus, L. arboreus, L. succulentus*) Alfalfa (*Medicago sativa*) Sweet White Clover (*Meliotus alba*) Vetches (*Vicia villosa, V. gigantea, V. americana*)
RANGE:	Throughout California (four subspecies) and the United States except the southern states.
NOTES:	Very closely related to the extinct Xerces Blue in San Francisco.

WESTERN PYGMY-BLUE ▶ *Brephidium exile*

KEY FIELD MARKS: A row of iridescent spots (without orange as in Acmon Blue) near the margin of the Under Hind Wing. Very small size.

SIZE: $^1/_2 - ^3/_4$

ADULTS FLY: March through September

HIBERNATE AS: Pupae

HOST PLANTS: Found near salt water marsh habitat.
Goosefoot family (*Chenopodiaceae*)
Beach Saltbush (*Atriplex leucophylla*)
Fat Hen (*Atriplex patula* v. *hastata*)
Lamb's Quarters (*Chenopodium album*)

RANGE: Throughout California (except the northwest counties) and the United States (except the north). Found near food plants around salt water marshes.

NOTES: This species, like the Acmon and the Western Tailed-Blue, moves its Hind Wings while nectaring to draw attention to its "eye spots."

GREENISH BLUE ▶ *Plebejus saepiolus*

KEY FIELD MARKS: Under Hind Wing with only one or two **small orange spots.**

SIZE: $7/8 - 1^{1}/4$

ADULTS FLY: April through August

HIBERNATE AS: Larvae

HOST PLANTS: Clovers (*Trifolium* spp.)

RANGE: Coast to mountains in California (not in the Central Valley and rare in southern California); northern and western North America.

Upper Wing of Male

Note the **wide** dark edges compared to *Lycaena heteronea* (Blue Copper, pictured on page 182).

ARROWHEAD BLUE ▶ *Glaucopsyche piasus*

KEY FIELD MARKS: Under Hind Wing has white triangles pointing downward toward the body.

SIZE: $1\frac{1}{8} - 1\frac{1}{4}$

ADULTS FLY: April through July

HIBERNATE AS: Pupae

HOST PLANTS: Lupines (*Lupinus* spp.)

RANGE: In California, on the north coast and in the high Sierra Nevada. Western United States. Photographed near Sonora Pass.

REAKIRT'S BLUE ▶ *Hemiargus isola*

KEY FIELD MARKS: Hind Wing with two to three iridescent spots; Under Front Wing has **band of dark spots** surrounded by white.

SIZE: $^7/_8 - 1$

ADULTS FLY: April through October

HIBERNATE AS: Pupae

HOST PLANTS: Acacia (*Acacia* spp.)
Honey Mesquite (*Prosopis glandulosa*)

RANGE: Desert and east of the Sierra Nevada; south-western United States. Migrates to large areas of the United States as far north as Canada.

NOTES: Recent research by Diane Wagner in southeastern Arizona has illuminated an intricate relationship between the larval and pupal stages of this butterfly and 13 species of ants, on the summer host plant *Acacia constricta*. The ants protect the larvae from predators and in return receive a sugary fluid from a gland on the back of the larvae. The fully formed larvae then travel into the nest of *one* of the 13 species of ants and pupate there. This gives them protection in a location two cm. underground. The ants tend the pupae. When the adult butterfly breaks out of the pupal shell, it has two minutes to exit the nest. Experiments show that after two minutes the ants will attack and kill the butterfly.

WESTERN TAILED-BLUE ▶ *Everes amyntula*

KEY FIELD MARKS: A Blue with a tail; one orange Under Hind Wing spot (sometimes a faint second spot).

SIZE: $1 - 1^{1}/_{4}$

ADULTS FLY: March through August

HIBERNATE AS: Mature larvae

HOST PLANTS: Pea (*Lathyrus* spp.)
Lotus (*Lotus* spp.)
Vetch (*Vicia* spp.)

RANGE: In California widespread but not in the Central Valley or the desert areas. Western North America.

NOTES: Very similar to the Eastern Tailed-Blue (*Everes comyntas*), which usually has at least **two** strong Under Hind Wing spots. Photographed at Sonora Pass.

GRAY HAIRSTREAK ▶ *Strymon melinus*

KEY FIELD MARKS: A small butterfly with **gray** Under Hind Wing, an orange band on both Under Front and Hind Wings, and two large orange spots at the base of the Hind Wing.

SIZE: 1 – 1¼

ADULTS FLY: March through October

HIBERNATE AS: Pupae

HOST PLANTS: Alfalfa (*Medicago sativa*)
Sweet Clover (*Melilotus alba*)
Clovers (*Trifolium tridentatum*, *T. repens*)
Cheeseweed (*Malva nicaensis*)
Coffeeberry (*Rhamnus californica*)

RANGE: Throughout California and North America.

NOTES: Butterflies in this group are called Hairstreaks because of their tendency to have tails, which are black tipped with white. These could be construed as "antennae" by a predator, and the bright spots as "eyes"; the lower apex of the Hind Wing is everted outward to look like a "head." By moving the back wings continuously while sipping nectar, the butterfly draws attention to the wrong end of its body. Bird predators take nips out of this part of the wing, thus allowing the butterfly to escape. Note also that the orange, black and white lines lead one's eye to this "head end."

GRAY HAIRSTREAK ▶ *Strymon melinus*

Upper Wing

Note the short and long tails on each wing, and compare with photograph on page 136.

Hairstreaks usually don't bask with the wings out like this. Rather, with wings together, they tilt to get the maximum direct sunlight.

Compare this photograph with those of the Swallowtails. Notice the similarity of deceit (the large "eye spots" and fake antennae).

COASTAL BRAMBLE (GREEN) HAIRSTREAK
▶ *Callophrys dumetorum viridis*

KEY FIELD MARKS: Under Front Wing practically all green; **white** fringe on edge of Under Wing.

SIZE: $1\frac{1}{8} - 1\frac{1}{4}$

ADULTS FLY: March through April (June)

HIBERNATE AS: Pupae

HOST PLANTS: Wide-leaved Buckwheat (*Eriogonum latifolium*)

RANGE: *C.d. viridis* has a narrow range near the coast from San Luis Obispo County to Mendocino County. However, the inland subspecies *C.d. dumetorum* is widespread over California and the western United States.

NOTES: Photograph is of *C.d. viridis* on its host plant. The inland subspecies has more **brown** and no white fringe on the Under Wing.

CALIFORNIA HAIRSTREAK ▶ *Satyrium californicum*

KEY FIELD MARKS: Under Hind Wing has a **blue spot** capped with **thin orange crescent.**

SIZE: $1^1/_8 - 1^3/_8$

ADULTS FLY: May through July

HIBERNATE AS: Egg

HOST PLANTS: California Lilac (*Ceanothus cuneatus*)
Valley Oak (*Quercus lobata*)

RANGE: Throughout California. West coast states and the central western states through Wyoming and Colorado.

HEDGEROW HAIRSTREAK ▶ *Satyrium saepium*

KEY FIELD MARKS: Under Hind Wing with a **blue spot not capped with orange**.

SIZE: $1 - 1^1/_8$

ADULTS FLY: April through July

HIBERNATE AS: Eggs

HOST PLANTS: California Lilac (*Ceanothus cuneatus*)

RANGE: Throughout California and east to Colorado. British Columbia to New Mexico and Baja.

NOTES: In this photograph, a tear in the butterfly's wing reveals the coppery color of the Upper Wing. Behr's Hairstreak also has coppery Upper Wing but has a much different Under Wing pattern (see page 152).

'NELSON'S' JUNIPER HAIRSTREAK
▶ *Callophrys gryneus nelsoni*

KEY FIELD MARKS: Under Hind Wing is brown with a **violet tint**; both Under Wings have a white line.

SIZE: $^{7}/_{8} - 1^{1}/_{8}$

ADULTS FLY: May through July

HIBERNATE AS: Pupae

HOST PLANTS: Incense Cedar (*Calocedrus decurrens*)

RANGE: Throughout California except the deserts; west coast states from Mexico to Canada.

WESTERN PINE ELFIN ▶ *Callophrys eryphon*

KEY FIELD MARKS: Under Hind Wing is irregularly banded; a zig-zag white submarginal vertical line on both wings; sharp-pointed brown cones beyond the zig-zag line.

SIZE: $1\frac{1}{8} - 1\frac{1}{4}$

ADULTS FLY: May through July

HIBERNATE AS: Pupae

HOST PLANTS: Ponderosa Pine (*Pinus ponderosa*)
Monterey Pine (*Pinus radiata*)
Bishop Pine (*Pinus muricata*)
Lodgepole Pine (*Pinus murrayana*)

RANGE: Throughout California but not in the Central Valley or desert areas. Widespread in the western United States and across the north from British Columbia to Maine.

BROWN ELFIN ▶ *Callophrys augustinus iroides*

KEY FIELD MARKS: No tail, but note the downward projection of the Hind Wing.

SIZE: 1 (exactly)

ADULTS FLY: February through April

HIBERNATE AS: Pupae

HOST PLANTS: Madrone (*Arbutus menziesii*)
Soap Plant (*Chlorogalum pomeridianum*)

RANGE: Throughout southwestern Colorado to California and southward for sub-species *iroides*.

BEHR'S HAIRSTREAK ▶ *Satyrium behrii*

KEY FIELD MARKS: Under Wing with small dark spots, each with a border of white on its **outer** edge.

SIZE: $1 - 1\frac{1}{4}$

ADULTS FLY: June through August

HIBERNATE AS: Eggs

HOST PLANTS: Antelope Brush (*Purshia tridentata*)
Waxy Bitter Brush (*Purshia glandulosa*), in southern California only

RANGE: Mostly east of the Sierra Nevada/Cascade Divide and in mountains in southern California.

GREAT PURPLE HAIRSTREAK ▶ *Atlides halesus*

KEY FIELD MARKS: Under Hind Wing has red and green markings; abdomen is **orange**.

SIZE: $1\frac{1}{4} - 1\frac{1}{2}$

ADULTS FLY: March through October

HIBERNATE AS: Pupae

HOST PLANTS: Common Mistletoe (*Phoradendron flavescens*)

RANGE: Most of California but rare in the north; found in the Southwest and in southern states.

NOTES: This individual has had a large bite taken out of its rear wings, again showing the efficacy of the Hairstreak strategy of producing a "false head" in the rear (see discussion on page 135).

LUSTROUS COPPER ▶ *Lycaena cupreus*

KEY FIELD MARKS: Under Front Wing **orange** with dark spots;
Under Hind Wing with a **relatively straight
orange** submarginal line.

SIZE: $1^{1}/_{8} - 1^{1}/_{4}$

ADULTS FLY: Late June to early August

HIBERNATE AS: Half-grown larvae

HOST PLANTS: Alpine Dock (*Rumex paucifolius*)
Sheep's Sorrel (*Rumex acetosella*)
Mountain Sorrel (*Oxyria digyna*)

RANGE: Sierra Nevada, Oregon Cascades, and the
Rocky Mountains.

NOTES: This species is highly attracted to Pussy Paws
(*Calyptridium umbellatum*) for a nectar source.

LUSTROUS COPPER ▶ *Lycaena cupreus*

Upper Wing

Showing **coppery red** with **black border** and **black spots**.

PURPLISH COPPER ▶ *Lycaena helloides*

KEY FIELD MARKS: Orange **crescents** near margin of Under
Hind Wing.

SIZE: $1 - 1^3/_8$

ADULTS FLY: April through October

HIBERNATE AS: Egg

HOST PLANTS: Docks (*Rumex* spp.)
Knotweeds (*Polygonum* spp.)

RANGE: Throughout California. Widespread from
northern Alaska to Baja California and
eastward to Ohio. Not in the southern states.

NOTES: This photograph shows the Under Wing of
the female.

PURPLISH COPPER ▶ *Lycaena helloides*

Female Upper Wing

Showing broad dark border (male Upper Wing is purplish, not orange).

RUDDY COPPER ▶ *Lycaena rubidus*

KEY FIELD MARKS: Upper Wing coppery but with **very faint dark spots**.

SIZE: $1\frac{1}{8} - 1\frac{1}{2}$

ADULTS FLY: July through August

HIBERNATE AS: Eggs

HOST PLANTS: Curly Dock (*Rumex crispus*)
Docks (*Rumex* spp.)

RANGE: Mostly east of the Sierra Nevada up to the crest in California; Oregon and Washington east to North and South Dakota, Nebraska, Colorado, and New Mexico.

NOTES: This photograph shows the Upper Wing of the male.

RUDDY COPPER ❯ *Lycaena rubidus*

Under Wing

Note the **nearly white** Under Hind Wing.

KEY FIELD MARKS: Upper Front Wing (female) is yellow orange
with a dusky border; Upper Hind Wing has
an **orange** border at the hind margin. (Male
Upper Wing is almost identical to Edith's
Copper; see page 174.)

SIZE: $1^{3}/_{8} - 1^{1}/_{2}$

ADULTS FLY: May through June

HIBERNATE AS: Eggs

HOST PLANTS: Curly Dock (*Rumex crispus*)
Fiddle Dock (*Rumex pulcher*)
Other Docks (*Rumex* spp.)

RANGE: Throughout California (rare in the north)
and portions of western Oregon.

GREAT COPPER ▶ *Lycaena xanthoides*

Female Under Wing

Note the **very short** tail (compare to Tailed Copper, pictured on page 176).

EDITH'S COPPER ▶ *Lycaena editha*

KEY FIELD MARKS: Under Hind Wing has roundish gray spots
(some with white border).

SIZE: $1^{1}/_{8} - 1^{1}/_{4}$

ADULTS FLY: Late June to August

HIBERNATE AS: Eggs

HOST PLANTS: Dusky Horkelia (*Horkelia fusca*)
Santa Rosa Horkelia (*Horkelia tenuiloba*)

RANGE: Sierra Nevada and Cascades of California.

EDITH'S COPPER ▶ *Lycaena editha*

Male Upper Wing

Showing a **brown color** with one orange crescent at the edge of the Upper Hind Wing.

TAILED COPPER ▶ *Lycaena arota*

KEY FIELD MARKS: Our only **tailed** Copper (Great Copper and Edith's Copper have only a slight hint of a tail). Under Hind Wing pattern much more complex than in Hairstreaks.

SIZE: $1^1/_8 - 1^3/_8$

ADULTS FLY: May through June

HIBERNATE AS: Eggs

HOST PLANTS: Currant and Gooseberry (*Ribes* spp.)

RANGE: Throughout California (except the Central Valley). Oregon to Baja, and east to Wyoming, Colorado, and New Mexico.

TAILED COPPER ▶ *Lycaena arota*

Showing the coppery **Upper Wing of the Male**, with orange crescents merging where the tail extends beyond the wing.

TAILED COPPER ▶ *Lycaena arota*

Showing the **Upper Wing of the Female**.

BLUE COPPER ▶ *Lycaena heteronea*

KEY FIELD MARKS:	Male Upper Wing very bright blue with **narrow** dark edge.
SIZE:	1¼
ADULTS FLY:	May through June
HIBERNATE AS:	Eggs
HOST PLANTS:	Buckwheat (*Eriogonum* spp.)
RANGE:	Throughout California (mostly in the northern portion of the Sierra Nevada). North to British Columbia and east to Montana, Wyoming, Colorado, and New Mexico.
NOTES:	This butterfly was originally classified as a Blue, but it flies more swiftly than Blues, and the body structures resemble Coppers'. In the Greenish Blue, the male's Upper Wing is very similar to this species' but has a much **broader** dark edge (see page 128).

BLUE COPPER ▶ *Lycaena heteronea*

The female's Upper Wing has spots (unlike any species of Blue), and its Under Hind Wing is **white** with **no** dots (or only a few).

LILAC-BORDERED COPPER ▶ *Lycaena nivalis*

KEY FIELD MARKS: Under Hind Wing has a **pinkish** cast on the outer portion; Under Front Wing **yellowish** with black spots.

SIZE: $1^1/_8 - 1^1/_4$

ADULTS FLY: June to August

HIBERNATE AS: Eggs

HOST PLANTS: Knotweeds (*Polygonium* spp.)
Douglas's Knotweed (*Polygonium douglasii*)

RANGE: Sierra Nevada/Cascades in California; northwestern United States.

PROPERTIUS DUSKYWING ▶ *Erynnis propertius*

KEY FIELD MARKS: Upper Front Wing has well-defined spots (especially the female's) and is heavily scaled with gray; Upper Hind Wing has light **tan** spots.

SIZE: $1^3/_8 - 1^1/_2$

ADULTS FLY: April through July

HIBERNATE AS: Full-grown larvae

HOST PLANTS: Coast Live Oak (*Quercus agrifolia*) Other Oaks (*Quercus* spp.)

RANGE: Throughout California. Also British Columbia to Baja California and northwestern Nevada.

NOTES: Skippers can be separated from other butterflies by the fact that the clubbed antennae are **bent backwards**. They also have excellent large eyes, stocky bodies, and powerful flight muscles. There are two groups of Skippers. The Spread-Wing Skippers (see this page through page 200) hold their wings out flat when perched (only occasionally folded over the body). The second group is the Grass Skippers (see pages 201-232).

MOURNFUL DUSKYWING ▶ *Erynnis tristis*

KEY FIELD MARKS:	Edge of **both sides** of the Hind Wing has a **white** border.
SIZE:	$1\frac{1}{8} - 1\frac{1}{4}$
ADULTS FLY:	March through October
HIBERNATE AS:	Larvae
HOST PLANTS:	Coast Live Oak (*Quercus agrifolia*) Blue Oak (*Quercus douglasii*) Valley Oak (*Quercus lobata*)
RANGE:	Throughout California except east of the Sierra Nevada. S1outhwestern United States to Texas.

NORTHERN CLOUDYWING ▶ *Thorybes pylades*

KEY FIELD MARKS: Upper Front Wing has three small **white spots** in the lower, inner area that form a **triangle**; Under Hind Wing has two irregular transverse dark bands.

SIZE: $1^3/_8 - 1^5/_8$

ADULTS FLY: May through July

HIBERNATE AS: Full-grown larvae

HOST PLANTS: Alfalfa (*Medicago sativa*)
False Indigo (*Amorpha californica*)
White Clover (*Trifolium repens*)
American Vetch (*Vicia americana*)
Lotus (*Lotus* spp.)

RANGE: Throughout California and most of the United States and southern Canada.

MEXICAN CLOUDYWING ▶ *Thorybes mexicana*

KEY FIELD MARKS: Upper Front Wing has **two rows of vertical white rectangles** connected by two horizontal spots.

SIZE: $1^1/_8 - 1^1/_4$

ADULTS FLY: June through August

HIBERNATE AS: Unknown

HOST PLANTS: Clover (*Trifolium* spp.)

RANGE: In California, the Sierra crest and eastward.

MEXICAN CLOUDYWING ▶ *Thorybes mexicana*

Under Wings of a mated pair showing two dark irregular bands.

SILVER-SPOTTED SKIPPER ▶ *Epargyreus clarus*

KEY FIELD MARKS: Under Hind Wing has a **large silver spot**; Upper Front Wing has a diagonal row of large dull yellow rectangles.

SIZE: $1^3/_4 - 2^1/_4$

ADULTS FLY: May through July

HIBERNATE AS: Pupae

HOST PLANTS: Wisteria (*Wisteria* spp.)
False Indigo (*Amorpha* spp.)
Black Locust (*Robina pseudo-acacia*)

RANGE: Throughout California except the Central Valley.

COMMON-CHECKERED SKIPPER ▶ *Pyrgus communis*

KEY FIELD MARKS: Upper Wing has extensive white markings on gray ground especially a row of **large white rectangles** in mid-wing.

SIZE: $1 - 1\frac{1}{8}$

ADULTS FLY: March through October (November)

HIBERNATE AS: Full-grown larvae

HOST PLANTS: Cheeseweed (*Malva nicaensis*)
Other Mallows (*Malva* spp.)

RANGE: Throughout California and all of United States and southwestern Canada, south to Argentina.

NOTES: The photograph shows a mating pair. The lighter-colored individual is the male. The darker one is the female.

WOODLAND SKIPPER ▶ *Ochlodes sylvanoides*

See pages 213-216 for Field Marks, etc.

The Grass Skippers use sedge and grass species for host plants. When perched they often hold the Hind Wings spread flat (90%) and the Front Wings spread only partly (45%). (See photo opposite). They also can hold their wings together over the body so that you see only the Under Hind Wing pattern.

This photograph shows the spread wing position. If you start from the yellow flower you see the Upper Hind Wing, the Under Front Wing, and the Upper Front Wing, each of which has a distinctive pattern.

COLUMBIAN SKIPPER ▶ *Hesperia columbia*

KEY FIELD MARKS: Under Hind Wing yellowish with a **mostly straight** silver (only slightly curved) spot band.

SIZE: $1^1/_8 - 1^3/_8$

ADULTS FLY: March through May, and September through October

HIBERNATE AS: Unknown

HOST PLANTS: June Grass (*Koeleria macrantha*)
California Oat Grass (*Danthonia californica*)

RANGE: California and Oregon. Not in the deserts.

NOTES: The fast, abrupt flight of the Skippers makes them difficult to follow. It is possible to locate one if you patiently watch while standing still. Keeping your eye on the spot where one lands, move **slowly** into closer range (or use close-focus binoculars).

Most individuals can be identified to species in the field by the marks of both Upper and Lower Wings. Knowing what patterns to look for on the Under Hind Wing is the key to beginning to sort out the species. The Columbian, Umber, Fiery, and Woodland have unique patterns and are arranged together here.

UMBER SKIPPER ▶ *Poanes melane*

KEY FIELD MARKS: Under Hind Wing has two large vague **yellowish** areas on rich umber brown.

SIZE: $1^1/_8 - 1^1/_4$

ADULTS FLY: March through June, and July through October

HIBERNATE AS: Unknown

HOST PLANTS: Hair Grass (*Deschampsia caespitosas*)
Bermuda Grass (*Cynodon dactylon*)

RANGE: California (rare in northern California) but not east of the Sierra Nevada.

UMBER SKIPPER ▶ *Poanes melane*

The Upper Front Wing has **four yellowish spots**; the bottom one is more of a streak. Note the characteristic backward hook on the antenna club, typical of Skippers.

FIERY SKIPPER ▶ *Hylephila phyleus*

KEY FIELD MARKS: Under Hind Wing has a yellowish ground color with **small roundish** dusky spots.

SIZE: $1\frac{1}{8} - 1\frac{1}{4}$

ADULTS FLY: April through December

HIBERNATE AS: Unknown

HOST PLANTS: Bermuda Grass (*Cynodon dactylon*)

RANGE: California (rare in the north) and Baja California, eastward to the Atlantic states and south to Argentina; also now a resident of Hawaii.

NOTES: This is a very common butterfly on golf courses and lawns. The antennae are very short compared to other similar Skippers.

FIERY SKIPPER ▶ *Hylephila phyleus*

Upper Front Wing of Males

The darkest shape in the middle of the left wing showing (Upper Front) is a gland called the **stigma**. Pheromones (external chemicals that elicit behavior in other members of the same species) are given off from the stigma to attract the female.

Note that the dusky shape just outside the stigma does not touch the stigma as in *Ochlodes sylvanoides* (next page).

Orange color on the edge of the wing extends deeply into the dark border, resembling flames. This is true of the Upper Hind Wing as well.

WOODLAND SKIPPER ▶ *Ochlodes sylvanoides*

KEY FIELD MARKS: On the Upper Front Wing the outer tip of the stigma directly touches a dusky mark which in turn almost touches the dusky outer border.

Note also that the dusky border of the Upper Hind Wing does not have deep orange intrusions as in the Fiery Skipper (page 212).

SIZE: $^7/_8 - 1^1/_8$

ADULTS FLY: July through October

HIBERNATE AS: Eggs or first-stage larvae

HOST PLANTS: Rye Grass (*Elymus* spp.)
Lawn Grasses

RANGE: Throughout California; British Columbia to Baja California, east to Alberta, south to Arizona and New Mexico.

WOODLAND SKIPPER ▶ *Ochlodes sylvanoides*

Under Hind Wings of a mated pair

Usually both sexes have a wide spot band, and the two upper spots are offset inwardly from the others (but sometimes the spot band is very faint or does not exist at all, as in this photograph).

COMMON BRANDED (DODGE'S) SKIPPER
▶ *Hesperia comma dodgei*

KEY FIELD MARKS: The Under Hind Wing has a white spot band that is curved (see photograph on next page) or that, because the bottom of the spot band is missing, may appear to be straight but diagonal (see photograph opposite); the ground color is chocolate brown.

SIZE: $1 - 1\frac{1}{4}$

ADULTS FLY: Late July through October

HIBERNATE AS: Eggs, larvae, or pupae

HOST PLANTS: Red Fescue (*Festuca tubra*)

RANGE: Many subspecies of *Hesperia comma* exist from Alaska to Labrador and south to Maine, Nebraska, and the western United States. The species complex is also common in Europe. Other subspecies than *dodgei* are found in various locations over most of California. Subspecies *dodgei* flies near the coast from Santa Cruz County through Marin County.

NOTES: This species is different from Rural, Sonoran, Sachem, and Sandhill Skippers in that the spots are **different** shapes and sizes.

COMMON BRANDED (DODGE'S) SKIPPER
▶ *Hesperia comma dodgei*

Under Hind Wing

Showing less commonly observed curved spot band in sub-species *dodgei*.

SONORAN SKIPPER ▶ *Polites sonora*

KEY FIELD MARKS: Under Hind Wing has a semicircular spot band in which all the spots are approximately the same size.

SIZE: $1 - 1^1/_4$

ADULTS FLY: July through September

HIBERNATE AS: Unknown

HOST PLANTS: Idaho Fescue (*Festuca idahoensis*)
Other grasses

RANGE: Not in the Great Basin. In the Coast Range from Sonoma County north and in the Sierra Nevada but not in the Central Valley or southern California. British Columbia to Baja California and east to Colorado.

NOTES: In this group (Sonoran, Rural, Sachem, and Sandhill), the outer spot band on the Under Hind Wing is more regular, and each spot is about the same size (Sandhill is the exception). The whole band pattern is shaped like the letter "C."

The photograph is of *Polites sonora sonora* (*P.s. siris* is much darker).

RURAL SKIPPER (FARMER) ▶ *Ochlodes agricola*

KEY FIELD MARKS: Upper Front Wing has **small clear spot**(s) above the stigma; not much orange below the stigma (compare with the Woodland Skipper, page 214).

Under Hind Wing has a very pale yellowish curved spot band; ground color orangish (see next page).

SIZE: $^7/_8 - 1$

ADULTS FLY: May through July

HIBERNATE AS: Unknown

HOST PLANTS: Grasses

RANGE: Throughout California and from southern Oregon to Baja California.

RURAL SKIPPER (FARMER) ▶ *Ochlodes agricola*

Under Hind Wing of the Male

Showing orangish ground color. The female often has an orange spot band accentuated by dusky coloration surrounding it.

SACHEM ▶ *Atalopedes campestris*

KEY FIELD MARKS:	Upper Front Wing of male (pictured here) has very large black stigma. Female has two **glassy** spots just outward from the middle dark spot.
SIZE:	1 – 1¼
ADULTS FLY:	April through June, and August through October
HIBERNATE AS:	Mature larvae
HOST PLANTS:	Bermuda Grass (*Cynodon dactylon*) St. Augustine Grass (*Stenotaphrum secondatum*) Kentucky Blue Grass (*Poa pratensis*) Red Fescue (*Festuca rubra*)
RANGE:	Throughout California and other parts of the United States.

SACHEM ▶ *Atalopedes campestris*

Under Hind Wing

Showing the curved spot band with a **faint brown area** just **inside** the lower part of the band (compare with the Under Hind Wing of the Sonoran Skipper, page 222).

SANDHILL SKIPPER ▶ *Polites sabuleti*

KEY FIELD MARKS: Under Hind Wing has irregular pale yellow spots that make a semicircular spot band, but the inner spots tend to be more **elongated** compared to the three previous Skippers; **yellow** veins extend to the edge of the wing (other Skippers have brown veins).

SIZE: $^7/_8 - 1$

ADULTS FLY: April through September

HIBERNATE AS: Pupae

HOST PLANTS: Salt Grass (*Distichlis spicata*)

RANGE: Throughout California as several named subspecies; British Columbia through Baja and east to Colorado and New Mexico.

PALE SWALLOWTAIL ▶ *Pterourus eurymedon*

Just as the eye spot of an adult Buckeye Butterfly may startle a young predator, the larva of the Pale Swallowtail (and Western Tiger Swallowtail) may startle their would-be predators with their magnificent fake eyes.

As shown in this photo, the larva holds on to a silken pad, which it spins for this purpose, to avoid accidently falling off the host plant. It will leave the silken pad to eat and then return. The pad also provides the larva with secure points of attachment for its legs when the creature is working to shed its skin during molts.

ANISE SWALLOWTAIL ▶ *Papilio zelicaon*

The Swallowtail larva has a forked *osmateria* (like a snake's tongue) that it quickly extrudes from its head when it is disturbed, giving off a foul smell.

PIPEVINE SWALLOWTAIL ▶ *Battus philenor*

When birds eat this larva they quickly vomit because of poisonous chemicals the larva obtains by eating the host plant (California Pipevine). The striking red and black coloration of the larva serves to remind experienced predators that this prey is to be avoided.

This photo is of the Arizona subspecies.

AMERICAN LADY ▶ *Vanessa virginiensis*

Many butterfly larvae, including all the Ladies (*Vanessa* spp.), spin a silken nest over themselves for protection against predators and parasitoids (wasps and flies that lay eggs on the larvae and subsequently kill their host by eating it from the inside). The American Lady larva eats the leaves of the host plant within this silk nest. As it enlarges and molts, it moves to another portion of the plant and builds a new protective nest.

WEST COAST LADY ▶ *Vanessa annabella*

The speed at which larvae develop depends mostly upon what part of the plant they are feeding on. Generally, larvae that feed on flowers pupate in two to three weeks; those that feed on leaves (as in this species), four to six weeks; root feeders take two months or more. This invididual was watched from the day the female laid the egg, and when photographed this last-stage larva was 45 days old.

Note the prominent yellow color on the back, which helps distinguish this species from the larvae of the Painted Lady (*Vanessa cardui*), which is predominantly **black** on the back.

VARIABLE CHECKERSPOT ▶ *Euphydryas chalcedona*

Knowledge of which plants a butterfly species eats (host plants) can be a big help when trying to identify larvae. The black and orange color of this larva is similar to the Common Buckeye (*Junonia coenia*), but for the most part the two species have different host plants. Also, this species has a **black** head while the Buckeye's is **orange**.

LORQUIN'S ADMIRAL ▶ *Limenitis lorquini*

Protective strategies that larvae have evolved include spines, silken nests, poisonous chemicals, large eye spots and, in this case, a particularly effective camouflage. Larvae of this species make an almost perfect imitation of a bird dropping. Not only does it look somewhat amorphous (including a hump in the front), but it mimics the white uric acid paste that covers typical bird fecal material. When resting, these larvae twist their heads and rear ends in opposite directions so that they do not line up with the rest of the body, further accentuating the camouflage.

MONARCH ▶ *Danaus plexippus*

The larva of this species, shown here eating a Milkweed seed pod, is generally poisonous to birds. Instead of camouflage (as in the Lorquin's Admiral), it advertises its presence with yellow, black, and white vertical bands, reminding predators that the last time they tried to eat this kind they vomited.

CALIFORNIA HAIRSTREAK ▶ *Satyrium californicum*

Here, ants are attending a California Hairstreak larva. Ants play important roles with many Hairstreaks, Blues, and Coppers in the larval stage, although the details have yet to be worked out in many species (but see Reakirt's Blue, page 131). Ants touch discrete parts of the larva, inducing it to give off honey dew near one of its rear segments. The honey dew, consisting of 18% sugar, is used by the ants. In return the ants protect the larva from predators and parasitoids.

BIBLIOGRAPHY

Cassie, et al., 1995. *North American Butterfly Association (NABA) Checklist and English Names of North American Butterflies.*

Garth, John S. and Tilden, J.W., 1986. *California Butterflies,* University of California Press.

North American Butterfly Association, 4 Delaware Road, Morristown, NJ 07960. New publication called *American Butterflies* started in 1993. $25/year.

Pyle, Robert M., 1981. *The Audubon Field Guide to North American Butterflies,* Alfred A. Knopf.

Pyle, Robert M., 1984. *Handbook for Butterfly Watchers,* Houghton Mifflin.

Scott, James A., 1986. *The Butterflies of North America,* Stanford University Press.

Steiner, John, 1988. *Butterflies of the San Francisco Bay Region, A County Species List.*

Tilden, J.W. and Smith, Arthur C., 1986. *Western Butterflies,* Peterson Field Guides, Houghton Mifflin.

INDEX

A

B

C